Disney's CHRISTMAS WITH ALL THE TRIMMINGS

ORIGINAL STORIES AND CRAFTS FROM MICKEY MOUSE AND FRIENDS

By KATHERINE APPLEGATE

Illustrated by PHIL WILSON

Disney PRESS

NEW YORK

For Lisa Franklin Leach, with love
—K. A.

A SAFETY NOTE

This book contains instructions and recipes for Christmas crafts and treats. Some of these involve cooking, cutting, and other activities that require an adult's guidance. So please be sure to have an adult help you.

For information address Disney Press, 114 Fifth Avenue, New York, New York 10011.
First Edition
1 3 5 7 9 10 8 6 4 2
Library of Congress Catalog Card Number: 93-74420
ISBN 0-7868-3003-4

TABLE OF CONTENTS

"This Christmas," said Mickey Mouse as he tied a big red bow around his mailbox, "is going to be the best Christmas ever." He stared dreamily at the clouds blanketing the sky like a thick gray quilt. A light snow was beginning to fall. "This year I'm going to pick out my own tree and chop it down myself, just like they used to in the good old days."

"Chop?" Donald Duck repeated. "Sounds like hard work. I'd better supervise."

"One good swing and *I'll* chop it down!" Goofy said. He pretended to swing an ax, but he swung so hard that he spun around, lost his balance, and landed in a holly bush.

"Maybe I should do the chopping," said Mickey with a smile as he helped Goofy to his feet. "I'll go get my ax. Donald, why don't you round up the boys while Goofy starts the jalopy?"

"Wait a minute," said Donald. "*I'm* supervising here." He turned to Goofy. "Goofy, you start the jalopy while I round up the boys and Mickey gets his ax."

Mickey had just walked in the door when the phone rang in the kitchen. "Merry Christmas Eve!" he answered.

"Mickey? It's me, Minnie!"

"Minnie!" Mickey exclaimed happily. "How's Aunt Minerva?"

"She's feeling much better. It was just her rheumatism acting up. The good news is I'll be coming home this afternoon."

"That's great!" Mickey said. "I've missed you so much, Minnie!" He gazed out the kitchen window across Mousehead Lake. The lake was a mile-wide circle with two little coves at one end, like a head with two ears. Aunt Minerva's cottage was between the ears, straight across the lake from Mickey's house. It was such a long way off that Mickey could barely make out the little cottage nestled among the pines with smoke corkscrewing out its chimney.

"I promise I'll be back as soon as I can," said Minnie.

"You'd better," Mickey said. "Christmas wouldn't be the same without you." He waved good-bye to Aunt Minerva's cottage as he hung up, even though he knew Minnie couldn't see him.

A few minutes later, everyone piled into Goofy's trusty old jalopy. Goofy sat in the driver's seat while Mickey and his nephews, Morty and Ferdie, crowded into the passenger seat. Donald sat in the back with his nephews, Huey, Dewey, and Louie. Pluto sat on Donald's lap and stuck his head out the window.

"I wish you'd let me drive," Donald grumbled. "I always get carsick when Goofy's behind the wheel. *I'm* a much better driver."

"How about that time you backed into the lake, Unca Donald?" asked Huey as Goofy started the engine. "Remember how we found a trout in the glove compartment?"

"Or that time you got the car stuck in reverse?" said Dewey. "We had to drive backward all the way home to Duckburg."

Louie laughed. "Or that time—"

"Quiet, Louie," said Donald sternly. "Goofy needs to concentrate."

"I know just the place to find the perfect tree," said Mickey. He gave Goofy directions, and before long they were surrounded by a dense green forest. Swaying pine trees stretched out their thick green boughs like long arms, catching tiny snowflakes before they could reach the earth.

"This is it," Mickey announced. He pointed to a carved wooden sign on the side of the road.

"Bartholomew Beaver's U-Cut Tree Farm," Ferdie read. *"I'm too pooped to chew, but you're in luck. Just chop your tree, and leave a buck."*

They found old Bartholomew holding a long stick over a little fire. "Ah, my favorite," Mickey said as he handed Bartholomew a dollar bill. "Toasted marshmallows."

"Toasted stick, actually," Bartholomew corrected him. He popped the stick in his mouth and chewed. "Cut any tree you want," he said. "But don't take too long. See the way the wind's picked up? Looks like a storm's brewing."

"Come on, gang," Mickey cried. "Somewhere out there our tree is waiting for us."

With the boys leading the way, the group set off through the tall trees. Already the forest floor was carpeted with a thin layer of snow.

Suddenly Louie stopped. "Look," he whispered in a hushed voice as Pluto sniffed the ground. "Bear tracks!"

Everyone gathered around the paw print Louie had found. "I think I'll go supervise from the car," said Donald.

"Relax, Donald," Mickey said. "We're just here to cut down a Christmas tree. What could go wrong?"

"We could end up as someone's Christmas Eve dinner, that's what could go wrong," Donald replied. "There are big furry things in this forest, Mickey. Big furry things with big furry appetites!"

Mickey started to answer, but at that moment he saw something that made him forget all about whatever he'd been about to say. It was a tree—the most perfect, most beautiful tree he'd ever seen.

"There it is," he whispered, pointing. "Our tree."

"It's tree-mendous!" Goofy exclaimed.

"Stand back, everybody," Mickey instructed. He started chopping away at the thick trunk. Then he paused to wipe his brow. "A couple more swings and I'll—"

"G-r-r-r!"

Mickey paused, his ax in midair. "Goofy," he asked nervously, "that *was* your stomach growling, wasn't it?"

"Not unless his stomach can climb trees," Donald said.

Everyone stared up at the tree. There, tucked in among the tree's branches, sat a little brown bear cub, hanging on to the trunk for dear life.

"Aww, hello there, little fella," said Mickey gently. "What are you doing up there in our Christmas tree?"

"Cute little guy, isn't he?" Goofy said. "Come on, furry fella."

Cautiously the bear climbed into Goofy's outstretched arms.

"Chop away, Uncle Mickey!" Ferdie cried.

Two more big swings and the tree tottered. Mickey and the boys gave it a final push. The cub clung to Goofy as the tree crashed to the ground.

Mickey gazed at the tree with satisfaction. "Gentlemen," he said proudly, "I give you the world's most perfect Christmas tree."

"G-G-R-R-R-R-R!!!"

Mickey whirled around. "Was that him, Goofy?" he asked, pointing to the little cub.

Goofy shook his head, eyes wide.

"Then who"—Mickey cleared his throat—"uh, was it?"

"G-G-R-R-R-R-R!!!"

Donald gasped. "Remember that story about the three bears?" he whispered. "Well, mama bear and papa bear just showed up. And I don't think they're looking for porridge!"

Mickey turned to see two huge bears lumbering toward them, sharp teeth glistening.

Goofy gulped nervously as he set the little cub on the ground. "Maybe they thought I was trying to bearnap the little fella," he said.

"I don't know," Donald replied. "I don't speak bear. And I'm not about to stick around and learn how. Let's run for it!"

"B-b-b-but our tree!" Mickey cried. "We can't leave without our tree!"

"We'll get an artificial one," Donald squawked. "Green. Gold. Purple with yellow spots. You name it. Now come *on*!"

But Mickey couldn't go, not without his beautiful tree. As the bears closed in, he struggled all alone to lift the big trunk.

"*G-R-R-R!!!*" the bears roared again, still ambling toward them.

Donald looked at Goofy. Goofy looked at Donald. "One-two-three—*lift*!" Donald cried. They each grabbed a branch, and the three friends lifted the big tree onto their shoulders as the boys watched anxiously.

"One-two-three—*run for it*!" Goofy added.

They dashed through the forest, weaving in and out through the maze of trees, slipping and sliding on the snow. Mickey thought he could hear something large hurrying along right behind them, but he didn't dare look back. He just kept a firm grip on the tree and kept going. Even when his hat—his very favorite, warmest red

hat—flew off his head, he didn't even think about stopping.

"Nice tree," said Bartholomew when they reached the clearing, panting and groaning. "But what's your rush?"

Mickey finally dared to glance back the way they'd come—just in time to see the three bears lope into the clearing. "Oh," said Bartholomew, ducking behind a bush. "*That's* your rush."

As the friends neared the jalopy, the father bear stood on his hind legs and lumbered closer, his huge paws slicing the air.

"G-G-G-R-R-R-R!!!" he roared.

"That's one *grrr* too many!" Donald shouted. Everyone dropped the tree and made a mad leap for the jalopy—except Mickey.

"Get in, Uncle Mickey, get in!" Ferdie cried.

"I am not giving up my tree," Mickey said in a trembling squeak of a voice. He looked up at the giant bear, who towered over him like a furry skyscraper. Mickey smiled meekly. "I mean, I am not giving up my perfect tree, Mr. Bear. Sir."

Mickey jumped into the front seat of the jalopy, leaving the door open so he could cling to the trunk of his tree.

"He's coming, Goofy!" Donald screamed. "And I think he wants a between-meal snack!"

"I don't suppose any of you have seen my key?" Goofy asked, frowning. "A little silver thing? You use it to start the car?"

Donald groaned. "Good-bye, cruel world!"

"Think, Goofy," Mickey urged. "Use your head!"

"My head?" Goofy repeated. "Good idea, Mickey. My head."

The bear dropped his great paws onto the roof of the car and shook the jalopy back and forth.

"Wow!" Morty exclaimed. "Like a roller coaster, only with sound effects!"

"And bear drool," Donald added.

"My head, my head," Goofy repeated thoughtfully.

"I *told* you I should have driven," Donald said as the father bear peered in through the window.

Suddenly Goofy's eyes lit up. "My *head!*" he exclaimed. He

reached under his hat and pulled out the key just as the bear poked his great paw through Mickey's open door.

Goofy floored the accelerator. The tires spun and squealed. They tore out of the clearing, but the road was slick with fresh snow, and the jalopy swerved back and forth and here and there.

"Hang on!" Goofy cried.

"I'm trying!" Mickey answered, clinging valiantly to his tree. The branches dragged on the snowy road like a giant broom, leaving behind a trail of green needles.

Ferdie looked out the back window. "You know, I think the baby bear has something red in his mouth," he said.

"It looks like Mickey's hat," Huey said.

"Good," Donald said. "They can eat that instead of us."

Suddenly the jalopy hit a patch of ice. "Look out for that tree!" Donald cried as they swerved straight toward a huge pine tree on the side of the road.

Goofy slammed on the brakes. The jalopy spun around and around in terrifying circles while Mickey hung on to his tree with all his might. Branches cracked and needles flew in the air, but still Mickey held tight to the trunk.

When they finally came to rest, all the boys cheered. "That was *better* than a roller coaster," Morty exclaimed. "Do it again, Goofy!"

Shaking and panting, Mickey got out of the jalopy. His hands burned from hanging on so tightly to the tree. His arms ached. He stared at his tree and sighed.

In the wild getaway ride, almost all the needles had fallen off.

"That's not a tree," said Donald. "That's a pine-scented skeleton."

By the time they reached Mickey's house, the roof and yard were covered with a glistening blanket of fresh snow. Together the friends dragged what was left of the tree inside and set it up in the living room.

"And to think we were nearly bear appetizers," said Donald, sinking into an easy chair. "Just so we could save that collection of twigs!"

"It's not *all* twigs," Mickey pointed out. "There are still a couple of needles left."

"We could paint it green," Goofy suggested.

"We could use it for kindling," Donald added.

"No," Mickey said firmly. "This is our tree. We picked it out. We chopped it down." Lovingly he touched a slender branch. "We risked our lives for it."

"But you said it was going to be the perfect tree," said Goofy. "And this one isn't exactly perfect, Mickey. Come to think of it, this one isn't exactly a tree."

"Well, I'll say one thing for it," Ferdie said. "It sure is the most *interesting* Christmas tree ever."

Mickey snapped his fingers. "You're right, Ferdie!" he cried. "I wanted a special tree, and you can't tell me this one isn't special. What counts is all the fun we had finding it."

Donald moaned. "You call that fun?"

"And we're going to have just as much fun decorating it," Mickey added. "We'll make our own ornaments, and by the time we're through, you won't even recognize it!"

For the next few hours, everyone helped make the ornaments. Mickey, Donald, and Goofy mixed and stirred and kneaded. The boys glued and painted. While they worked, they all drank warm apple cider and sang carols.

At last the ornaments were ready, and it was time to decorate the tree. Mickey wound colored lights around the bare twigs. Goofy followed behind, draping popcorn chains and tinsel everywhere.

The boys followed him, carefully hanging their homemade ornaments until every single branch was covered.

Donald, of course, supervised.

When every last inch of tree was decorated, they all stepped back to admire their handiwork.

"Not bad," said Donald. "For a great big twig."

"I believe I have a way with tinsel," Goofy said.

"I especially like our ornaments," said Louie.

Mickey sighed contentedly and smiled. Maybe it wasn't exactly the tree he'd imagined—but no one could argue that it wasn't the most unusual, most original, most interesting tree they'd ever had.

Mickey's Macaroni Snowflakes

BEFORE MICKEY BEGINS, HE NEEDS THE FOLLOWING ITEMS:

4 ice-cream sticks for each star
Glue
Assorted uncooked pasta
  (wheels, shells, ruffles,
  bows, corkscrews)
Gold or silver spray paint
  (or any nontoxic water-based
  paint and a paintbrush)
Ornament hooks

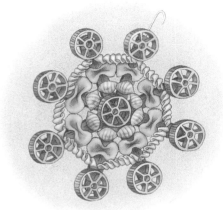

HOW MICKEY MAKES A SNOWFLAKE:

1. Mickey dabs some glue in the center of an ice-cream stick. Then he glues another stick on top of it, making an "X". He glues on two more sticks to form an eight-pointed "snowflake."

2. While he waits for the glue to dry, Mickey picks out his favorite pasta shapes and plans the way he'll glue them to his snowflake (he's especially fond of seashell-shaped pasta).

3. When his sticks are dry, Mickey applies a thick layer of glue to the front of his snowflake sticks.

4. One by one, starting at the center, he places his pasta on the sticks, laying them end to end.

5. When the glued pieces are dry, Mickey paints them.

6. When the paint is dry, Mickey turns the star over, places a drop of glue at the top of one of the ice-cream sticks, and glues an ornament hook into place. (Sometimes he ties on a bright string instead.)

Donald's Dough Ornaments

(Remember: these look good enough to eat, but they're just for the tree!)

BEFORE DONALD BEGINS, HE NEEDS THE FOLLOWING ITEMS:

1 cup salt

4 cups unsifted flour

1½ cups water

Bowl

Rolling pin

Wax paper

Cookie cutters

Small paper clips

Instant tea (optional)

Brushes and nontoxic paint or felt-tip pens

Clear gloss enamel (optional)

HOW DONALD MAKES HIS ORNAMENTS:

1. Donald mixes together the flour and salt in a bowl.

2. He adds the water, using his hands to mix the dough.

3. Donald kneads the dough, squishing it with his hands until it's nice and smooth and soft.

4. Next Donald pulls off a small ball of dough. With a rolling pin, he rolls out the dough on a piece of wax paper until the dough is about ¼ inch thick.

5. Donald cuts out shapes with his cookie cutters. He puts a paper clip into the back of each ornament to form a hook.

6. For a nice brown color on his ornaments, Donald mixes a little instant tea in warm water. Then he brushes the ornaments very lightly with the tea mixture.

7. Donald puts his ornaments on a cookie sheet. He bakes them in an oven set at 300 degrees for about an hour or until the ornaments are hard. Then he allows the ornaments to cool.

8. Now comes the best part—Donald and his friends paint their ornaments! (Sometimes, when the paint is dry, they brush on clear gloss enamel for extra shine.)

ookie dough!" Mickey exclaimed that afternoon, dipping his finger into a big bowl that Ferdie was stirring. "My favorite!"

"Get that finger out of there," Donald squawked, waving a rolling pin over his head. "We won't have any cookies if you don't stop eating everything in sight. Can't you see we're trying to create a culinary masterpiece here?"

"Gee, I thought we were baking cookies," Goofy said.

"You call *that* a cookie?" Donald demanded, pointing to a huge round piece of dough near Goofy.

"I'm making a cookie pizza," Goofy said proudly.

Just then the phone rang. Mickey smiled when he heard Minnie's voice. "Hi, Minnie!" he said. "What time are you getting here? We're baking cookies, and we found a beautiful tree. But we miss you."

"I miss you, too, Mickey," Minnie said wistfully. "But the road to Aunt Minerva's house is covered with snow, and I have to wait until they plow it."

"Don't worry, I'm sure you'll be on your way home soon," Mickey said confidently. "It can't keep snowing forever!"

He hung up the phone and gazed out the window at the lake.

The wind made little white waves on the water. Mickey could barely see Aunt Minerva's cottage through the snowflakes dancing across the sky in a graceful waltz.

"Is something wrong, Uncle Mickey?" Morty asked.

"Minnie is snowed in for a little while," Mickey said. "But I'm sure she'll be here soon. After all, Christmas wouldn't be Christmas without Minnie!" Mickey reached for a cookie cutter. "Minnie's going to be so surprised when she sees all the cookies we've made."

"She'll be surprised if there are any left," said Donald, snatching away the bag of nuts Goofy was munching.

A few nuts fell to the floor, and Pluto ran to eat them. He was always happy to clean up when Mickey and the others dropped things. He liked it best when they dropped cookies, of course, but there wasn't anything he wouldn't eat—except maybe radishes.

"Attaboy, Pluto," said Mickey. "My furry old garbage disposal."

Pluto was always glad to be of assistance. He wagged his tail so hard he knocked over a bag of flour and sent it flying across the room—right into Donald.

"That does it!" Donald cried. "Why don't you go bury a bone or something, Pluto?"

But Pluto wasn't interested in leaving—not when Goofy was just taking a fresh batch of cookies out of the oven. To get a better sniff, Pluto jumped up, planting his front paws on Goofy. Suddenly Goofy lost his balance. He spun

around and the cookies went airborne, whizzing through the air in a sugary blizzard.

"Pluto!" Mickey scolded.

Pluto hung his head. He didn't really see the problem. Personally, he preferred dining on the floor.

"I think you'd better go out to your doghouse until we're finished," said Mickey gently.

"Too many cooks spoil the broth. Especially when they're *dogs*!" Donald added.

With his tail between his legs, Pluto slunk through his doggy door into the icy cold. Instantly he missed the cozy warmth of the crowded kitchen, but he wasn't about to go back yet. He'd wait a while until they really missed him. Let Donald try licking up the floor and see how well he did. Floor licking was an art. Not just anybody could do it.

Pluto leaped off the porch steps into a pile of snow that came all the way up to his chin. He crossed the yard and was just about to

enter his doghouse when he noticed two bright, blinking eyes looking out at him from the dark interior.

Pluto jumped back in terror, burying himself in a snowdrift.
Then he remembered: He was a brave, fearless watchdog. If there
was a wild beast in his doghouse, it was his job to get rid of it. He
had to protect Mickey and the others—even if they *had* kicked him
out of the kitchen.

Pluto pawed his way out of the drift. He was covered in snow,
but that, he decided, was a good disguise. Wily watchdogs often
used disguises. Nearing his doghouse, he sniffed the air. No doubt
about it. There was something suspicious in his house, some horri-
ble, gigantic, dog-eating beast.

Pluto growled his most frightful growl and leaped his most
amazing leap. Into the dark recesses of his doghouse he bounded.
He growled again, even louder. Would it pounce? Bite? Snarl and
snort? Pluto waited for the beast to make its move.

And then it did. It licked Pluto, right on his snow-covered nose.

Pluto was a brilliant watchdog. He was ready for anything.
Anything but a noselick.

He yelped and hightailed it out the doorway, leaping to the top of his doghouse roof.

When it seemed safe, Pluto leaned down and peeked through the doorway. His long ears grazed the snow. Just then the beast peeked out. Its nose touched Pluto's.

Pluto sniffed. The beast sniffed back. Slowly it made its way out of the doghouse. But it wasn't a dog-eating beast.

It was a puppy! A tiny, shivering puppy. Pluto jumped off his roof to say hello. He gave the pup a friendly lick and a nice-to-meet-you tail wag, and she jumped up and down and backward and forward and inside and out, as if she'd never been so happy to see someone in her whole puppy life.

What was she doing out, lost and alone, on Christmas Eve? Pluto checked to see if she was wearing one of those fancy necklaces with her name engraved on it. Nope. No ID. Nothing.

The pup whimpered softly, looking up at Pluto with her big round eyes. Pluto knew that look. He used it on Mickey at the dinner table when he wanted leftovers. Gently he nudged the puppy

back into the doghouse. This was probably the little pup's first Christmas, and it was Pluto's job, as senior dog, to make it special. He was going to give her a Christmas surprise she'd never forget.

Pluto went back to the porch and peeked through his doggy door. Everyone was gazing at a pan full of very well-done cookies. "These cookies are burned to a crisp," Donald muttered. "Goofy, I told you to bake them for nine minutes!"

"I thought you said *ninety* minutes," said Goofy.

"I like them," Mickey said, taking a bite.

"And they'll make great hockey pucks," Goofy added.

Pluto slunk into the room. On the edge of the table sat two plates of beautiful cookies, already covered with sweet icing. Pluto stood on his hind legs, paws splayed on the tabletop, and picked up one of the plates in his mouth. It was heavy, heavier than the heaviest bone, but he managed to sneak it out his doggy door without dropping a crumb.

Meanwhile, Mickey and the gang were putting the finishing touches on the latest batch of sugar cookies. Then Mickey carried the plate of festively decorated cookies over to the kitchen table. "That's strange," he said as he set it down. "I thought this was our third batch of cookies."

"It is," said Donald.

"But there are only two plates here. Where's the other one?" Mickey asked.

Donald marched over and gasped. "Goofy!" he cried.

"I didn't eat them," Goofy protested. "Well, OK, maybe I ate one. Or two. Or three. But not *all* of them. I promise."

"It seems to me we had this same problem last Christmas," Donald said accusingly in his best detective voice. "You have the history. You had the opportunity." He poked at Goofy's stomach. "And you certainly had the motive!"

"It wasn't me!" Goofy protested.

"And it wasn't me," Mickey said. "So who ate them?"

"It could have been anyone," Goofy said. He looked over at

Huey, Dewey, and Louie. "See? They have crumbs all over them."

"It wasn't us!" Louie cried. "How about Morty and Ferdie? They have frosting all over their mouths!"

"We're innocent!" Ferdie cried. "Maybe it was your uncle Donald."

Everyone turned to look at Donald. "ME?" he screeched. "The head honcho? The supreme supervisor? The big boss?"

"How dare you accuse Unca Donald!" Dewey cried. He reached into the bowl in front of him and formed a dough snowball. Then he took aim and threw it straight at Ferdie.

SPLAT! Ferdie took a direct hit on the nose. He licked it off, then grabbed a handful of dough and aimed it at Dewey.

"Fire when ready!" Morty cried.

"Boys!" Mickey protested.

"Truce!" Donald yelled.

Ferdie threw the dough, but Dewey was too quick. He ducked just in the nick of time. Unfortunately, Donald didn't.

SPLAT! The dough landed right between Donald's eyes.

"Mmm," Donald said, taking a taste. "Not bad." With that, everyone started making dough snowballs.

Just then, Pluto poked his nose through his doggy door. His eyes went wide. Cookie dough was flying through the air. It landed on the floor, the ceiling, the cupboards, and the boys. It landed in Mickey's ears and on Donald's feet and in Goofy's wide-open mouth. It was wonderful to behold. It was going to require hours of professional floor licking.

But right now Pluto had a mission to complete. While everyone raced around the room, Pluto returned to the kitchen table. He didn't even have to slink this time. Everyone was having too much fun with the dough-ball fight to notice him.

Pluto grabbed another plate of cookies and slipped out the door. A moment later he returned for the last plate. Outside again, he trotted over to the little pine tree in the center of Mickey's lawn. He set down the plate beside the others and picked up a cookie between his teeth, careful not to crunch it. It took all his willpower not to eat it, but he reminded himself that he wanted to use every cookie in his surprise for his new friend.

Pluto stood up on his hind legs, bracing himself with his paws. Then, ever so gently, he placed the cookie on top of a branch. One by one, Pluto arranged the rest of the cookies on the branches of the little tree. When he was finished, he stepped back to admire his work. It was wonderful, almost as wonderful as Mickey's tree. And this tree was good enough to eat.

Inside the kitchen, everyone sat on the floor, laughing and panting and scraping dough off their faces. "Boy, I wish Minnie could have been here," Mickey said. "That sure was fun."

Suddenly Donald stopped licking the dough off his face. "The rest of the cookies!" he squawked. "They've disappeared!"

"This time we know it wasn't us," Mickey pointed out. "We were all too busy cookie *fighting* to be cookie *eating*."

"That leaves one suspect," Donald said. He dashed to the door and swung it open. "Pluto!" he shouted. "You—you canine cookie crook! You—"

Suddenly Donald stopped in midsquawk. He shook his head. Then he began to smile, a huge, amazing, face-stretching smile. "Come here, everyone," he said quietly. The others, curious, joined him in the doorway.

There, in the middle of the yard, sat a little pine tree, each of its branches laden with one of the missing cookies. "But why would Pluto decorate a tree out here?" Huey whispered.

Just then, Pluto emerged from his doghouse, followed by a tiny, bouncing puppy. He cleared a path through the snow for the pup and led her to the pine tree. The puppy looked up at Pluto expectantly, as if to ask, For me?

Pluto gave her a little nudge with his nose. The puppy's eyes went wide. She danced around the tree, barking and jumping, her tail a blur. She reached up to the first branch, grabbed a cookie in her mouth, and munched it down. Then she dashed over to Pluto to give him a thank-you face lick.

Mickey ran over and gave Pluto a hug. "You sure are a good old guy, you know that?" Pluto wagged his tail. He did know, but still, it was nice to hear sometimes.

The puppy galloped over to Mickey and leaped into his arms. "Hey, girl," Mickey said. "Don't you have a family of your own? Why don't you come inside and spend Christmas with us?"

Pluto licked Mickey on his nose to tell him that he sure was a nice old guy, too.

When they were all back inside, Mickey looked at his dough-splattered kitchen. "Well, this isn't exactly what I had in mind when we set out to bake cookies," he said. Then he looked out the window at the little cookie tree. "Actually," he added, giving Pluto another hug, "this is even *better* than what I had in mind."

Mickey watched as a pair of doves landed in the top branches and started pecking at the cookies Pluto and the puppy had left. "Maybe later we could make some other treats for the birds," he suggested. "I'm sure they'd like birdseed better than cookies."

"We should give the puppy a name," Dewey said.

"She's a Christmas puppy," said Donald. "Why don't we call her Noel?" The little puppy ran to Donald and licked his foot. "I think she likes me," he said.

"I think she likes that dough on your foot," said Goofy.

Donald gave Noel an affectionate pat and cleared his throat. "All right, gang, cleanup time!" he yelled. "I'll supervise!"

Pluto didn't have to be told what to do. He gave his new friend a nudge and began to instruct her in the fine art of professional floor licking.

After all, he was always glad to be of assistance.

Pluto's Peanut Butter Pinecones

BEFORE PLUTO BEGINS, HE NEEDS THE FOLLOWING ITEMS:

Pinecones
Birdseed (a small bag
    will be enough for
    several cones)
Yarn or string
Peanut butter (any kind)
1 large spoon
1 long pan or cookie sheet
1 plate

HOW PLUTO MAKES THE PINECONES:

1. While Pluto supervises, Mickey pours a layer of birdseed into the pan.

2. Mickey ties a piece of yarn around the top third of a pinecone and makes a knot.

3. Next, he scoops up a spoonful of peanut butter and spreads it over the pinecone. He repeats this until the cone is completely covered. (If his hands get too peanut-butter-y, Pluto helps by licking them off. But *you* can wash your hands in the sink!)

4. Mickey places the pinecone in the pan of birdseed.

5. Now Pluto gets to help. He rolls the peanut butter pinecone back and forth in the birdseed. (Pluto uses his nose, but you can use your hand.)

6. Mickey places each seed-covered pinecone on a plate.

7. When all the cones are ready, Pluto leads Mickey to his favorite tree. Mickey ties the cones to the tree branches.

8. Mickey and Pluto go back inside and watch from the window as the birds and squirrels discover the wonderful treats!

Goofy's Deep-Dish Cookie Pizza

BEFORE HE BEGINS, GOOFY NEEDS THE FOLLOWING ITEMS:
1 spoon
Bowls
Plastic wrap
2 cake pans

FOR THE COOKIE PIZZAS (makes two):
1½ cups powdered sugar
2 sticks (1 cup) butter or margarine
1 teaspoon almond extract
1 teaspoon vanilla extract
1 egg
2⅓ cups all-purpose flour
1 teaspoon baking soda
1 teaspoon cream of tartar

FOR THE FROSTING:
3 cups powdered sugar
1 stick (½ cup) softened butter or margarine
1 teaspoon vanilla extract
Approximately 2 to 3 tablespoons milk
Assorted fun toppings (candy, coconut, nuts, chocolate chips)

HOW GOOFY MAKES THE "PIZZA":

1. In a bowl, Goofy mixes together the powdered sugar, butter, almond extract, vanilla, and egg until smooth. Then he mixes in the rest of the ingredients.

2. Goofy divides the mixture into two bowls. He covers the bowls with plastic wrap and puts them in the refrigerator to cool for two to three hours.

3. Now Goofy heats his oven to 375 degrees. He lightly greases two standard cake pans.

4. Goofy presses the dough into each pan. Then he bakes them approximately nine minutes or until the cookie is lightly browned. He takes them out and lets them cool.

5. To make his icing, Goofy mixes the powdered sugar and butter together. He stirs in the vanilla and just enough milk to make the icing nice and smooth. (Goofy especially likes to lick the icing bowl when he's done.)

6. Goofy uses the frosting to ice the two cooled cookie pizzas. Then he tops them with lots of candy and goodies. When he's done he has two very sweet, very big deep-dish Christmas cookie pizzas!

I've never seen a storm like this," Goofy said that evening. "You'd think the clouds would run out of snow."

Mickey gazed out the window. "I wish Aunt Minerva had a boat," he said. "Then Minnie could row across the lake."

"Are we really snowed in?" Dewey asked.

"I'm afraid so," Mickey said. "We're snowed in, and Minnie's snowed out. The road to Aunt Minerva's is closed."

"Cool!" Louie cried. "We're trapped!"

Mickey laughed. "Not for long. By tomorrow morning the roads should be clear so Minnie and Aunt Minerva and all our friends can come over here to open presents."

"Presents!" Morty cried. "What if Santa can't make it here in all this bad weather?"

"He'll make it," said Mickey confidently. "Santa always makes it." He stared at the snow-filled sky. "What a great job," he said wistfully, "flying around the world in a reindeer-drawn sleigh."

"Give me your jalopy any day," said Donald. "It has a radio."

"And a roof," Goofy added.

Mickey yawned. "I've got one more present to wrap, then I'm off to bed. Boys, did you leave out some cookies and milk for Santa?"

"Yes, but Noel ate them," Ferdie said. "So we put some more on the mantel."

"See you bright and early Christmas morning," Mickey said. "Not *too* early, though." He grabbed a handful of cookies and headed up the stairs with Pluto and Noel.

Mickey went to his closet and got out his present for Minnie—a pair of beautiful shiny new ice skates. Minnie loved to skate, so Mickey was sure they were the perfect gift for her. Someday he hoped he could have a pair of skates, too, so Minnie could teach him. Of course, the lake wasn't frozen yet—it was too early in the winter—but with luck, it might freeze in the next couple of months.

Mickey took out some of the wrapping paper he and the boys had made that evening and carefully wrapped the skates while Pluto and Noel played tug-of-war with the ribbon. While he wrapped, he ate some more cookies, sharing a few with Pluto and the puppy.

"Not bad," Mickey said when he had finished. The ribbon was a little mangled, but he knew Minnie wouldn't mind.

Mickey rubbed his stomach. It was just possible that he'd eaten a few too many cookies. He crawled into bed with a sigh and thought about the day. If only Minnie had been here for their tree adventure and their cookie fight! She'd missed all the fun.

Outside the snow hung in the air like a lacy curtain. Mickey could just make out the lights of Aunt Minerva's cottage across the cold black water. He searched the skies. Was Santa already flying through the clouds, his sleigh laden with gifts?

"Good night," Mickey whispered to Pluto and Noel. "Sweet dreams." He closed his eyes and snuggled deep into his pillow.

Suddenly he felt someone shaking his shoulder hard. "Wake up, Mickey," came a low voice, followed by a very loud sneeze.

Mickey's eyes flew open. He flipped on his bedside light. There, sitting on the end of his bed, was Santa Claus! In the corner of the room sat one of Santa's elves, holding a box of tissues and tapping his foot impatiently.

"Santa?" Mickey whispered.

"Well, I'm not the Easter Bunny, that's for sure," Santa said with a chuckle that was interrupted by a loud sneeze. He blew his nose, a loud honk that woke Pluto and Noel.

Pluto growled. "Pluto," Mickey whispered nervously. "If you want a bone in your stocking, you'd better be nice."

Santa sneezed again, and the elf handed him a tissue. "Thank you, Elvis," Santa said.

"That cold sounds pretty bad, Santa," said Mickey sympathetically.

"It's a whopper," said Santa. "That's why I'm here. I want you to fill in for me."

"Fill in?" Mickey cried. "You mean . . . tonight? Christmas Eve?"

"No, he wants to know if you're free on March thirteenth." Elvis sighed. "*Told* you we should have asked the loudmouth."

"Loudmouth?" Mickey repeated.

"You know . . . the one who's always squawking about something or other."

Mickey smiled. "Oh. You must mean Donald."

"I know it's a lot to ask, Mickey," Santa said, "and I wouldn't bother you except that I . . . I . . . I . . . *a-choo!*"

Mickey couldn't believe his luck. "Of course I'll help!" he exclaimed. "Do I get to drive your sleigh?"

Santa nodded. "Ahem," said Elvis.

"With a little help from our reindeer staff," Santa added.

"And deliver presents to all the kids in the world?"

Santa nodded. "Ahem," said Elvis.

"With a little help from our hardworking elves," Santa added.

"When do I start?" Mickey asked, leaping out of bed.

Santa smiled. "Thanks, Mickey," he said gratefully. "You're a good sport." He took off his red cap and plopped it onto Mickey's head. "Good luck. And remember to watch that chimney at two-thirty-one East Main in Chattanooga. It's a little tight on the way down." He tugged at his beard. "And there's a dog in Britain who bites if you surprise him. A beagle. Just give him a tummy rub and you'll be fine."

Mickey frowned. "That's a challenging chimney in Chattanooga, a biting beagle in Britain—"

Santa climbed into Mickey's bed and snuggled in next to Pluto and Noel. He closed his eyes and began to snore before Mickey could ask him any more questions.

"I'll do a good job, Santa," Mickey said as confidently as he could. "I promise not to let you down."

"Take my hand and don't let go," Elvis interrupted.

Mickey nodded nervously. "Now, spell mistletoe backward," Elvis instructed.

"*E-O-T-E-L-T-S-I-M*," Mickey whispered.

He closed his eyes, and before he knew it, he and Elvis were swooshing through the window and out into the snowy night sky.

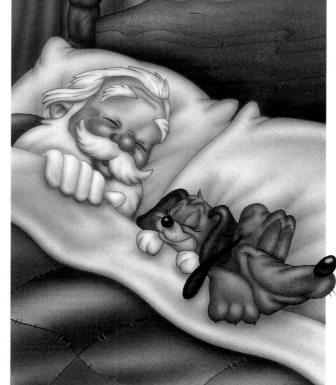

"We're there," Elvis announced as they came to a gentle landing on a flat, treeless expanse of snow.

An elf came rushing to meet them. He was wearing a red-and-green cap and a worried expression. "Where's Santa?" he demanded.

"Change in plans. Mickey here is filling in," said Elvis. "Mickey, this is Elvin. He's in charge of our toy inventory."

Elvin turned to Mickey. "Look, I hate to throw this at you first thing, but we've got a major problem on our hands."

"Problem?" Mickey echoed. He glanced around at the scurrying elves, who were bustling purposefully to and fro between huge warehouses made of glistening ice.

"Doll recall," said the elf. "We came this close to sending out twenty thousand Little Miss Dimples with their heads on backward. I've got all my elves working overtime on the head twisting, but it's going to take time." Elvin rubbed his temples. "And that's not all."

Mickey gulped. This was starting to sound a little more complicated than he'd imagined. "Is something else wrong?"

"You might as well see this yourself," Elvin said. He led Mickey and Elvis past a little white house with a sparkling tree in the front window.

"That's the Claus residence," Elvis explained.

"Look in the backyard," Elvin said.

Mickey peered around the back of the house and gasped. There,

dangling in the air, were all of Santa's reindeer, tangled up in a clothesline!

"What happened?" Elvis cried.

"We were practicing a new landing formation," said one of the reindeer.

"As you may have noticed, it didn't work," said another, who was gently swaying in the breeze. "Thanks to Mrs. Claus's clothesline."

"Do you think you guys could get us down from here?" asked the first reindeer. "This is really rather embarrassing. I mean, we're *professionals*."

Elvis shimmied to the top of one clothesline pole while Elvin climbed up the other. They began untying the rope attached to the poles.

"Wait!" one of the reindeer said. "We're going to—"

But it was too late. The rope came untied, and all the reindeer plummeted into a huge snowdrift below.

Slowly their snow-covered heads emerged from the drift. "I haven't been this humiliated since that Christmas we landed in a swamp in Florida," grumbled one of the reindeer.

"At least that was an honest mistake," said another, shaking snow off his antlers. "It looked like solid ground from a thousand feet up."

For the next half hour, Mickey, Elvis, and Elvin worked to untangle the reindeer. They had just freed the last one when two elves came sliding through the snow toward Mickey.

"Hey, are you the new Santa?" one of the elves asked. Mickey nodded.

"Here's your suit," the elf said, stuffing a huge red suit and a pair of black boots into Mickey's hands. "Hmm," he murmured. "Scrawny little guy, aren't you?"

"And here's your map," said the other elf, dropping a thick sheaf of paper at Mickey's feet. "There's one little glitch, though. Mrs. Claus's pet goat ate most of New Zealand and the coast of California for dinner."

"But how will I—"

"Just fly low and cross your fingers," said the elf.

With a heavy sigh, Mickey headed back to his sleigh. He tried on his new boots. Elvis was right. Mickey was going to have a hard time filling them.

He'd promised Santa that everything would be fine, but now he wasn't so sure he could deliver on his promise. As a matter of fact, he wasn't sure he could deliver much of anything. He had tangled reindeer, a well-munched map, and dolls with hair where their faces should be—

"You the Santa stand-in?"

Mickey looked down to see an elf carrying a huge stack of computer printouts—a stack nearly as tall as Mickey himself. "That's me," Mickey said. "What are those?"

"Your gift list," said the elf.

Mickey stared in disbelief at the first page of names, line after line of hopeful boys and girls, all waiting for him to make their wishes come true. "*All* these names?" he whispered.

"Oh, no."

"That's a relief," Mickey said with a sigh. "For a minute there I thought—"

"No, that's just the first stack. There are nine more."

Mickey gasped. He'd never manage to get to all these houses! Oh, how he wished he was back in his warm, cozy bed with Pluto and Noel, waiting for Santa to come to *them*.

When at last the sleigh was loaded and all the reindeer were hitched up, Mickey waved good-bye and picked up the reins.

"Good luck," yelled Elvis. "And don't forget to turn right at the North Star!"

Mickey felt a wave of panic. What if he failed, even after all the elves' hard work? He couldn't let Santa down!

Suddenly the sleigh began to move. "You'll do fine!" Elvis called as the sleigh swept into the cold night air and the elves waved good-bye. He turned to Elvin and shook his head grimly. "Santa should have asked the loudmouth," he said.

Below Mickey the night clouds swirled. Above him the stars lit the way like a sparkling highway.

"So," one of the reindeer called, "where to?"

Mickey swallowed past a lump in his throat. How did Santa do it? Work from north to south? East to west? Start with the kids who'd been nicest all year?

"How about we start with your neighborhood, to make it easy on you?" another reindeer suggested. "We'll work from there."

They veered to the right, and in the blink of an eye, there they were, right on top of Mickey's own house.

Mickey stepped out onto the slippery roof. He searched through his huge bag of gifts. Moments ticked by.

"You'd better hurry," one of the reindeer urged. "It's nearly dawn."

Dawn? Mickey gasped in dismay. He hadn't even gone to one house yet, and it was almost morning! Frantically he dug through his bag until he found the right gifts. "Now what?" Mickey asked the nearest reindeer.

"Go ring the doorbell," the reindeer replied.

Mickey started across the roof. "No, no!" the reindeer called. "Just a little on-the-job humor. Climb down the chimney."

Mickey peered down the dark hole. "What if I get stuck?"

"Santa made it last year, and let's face it, he'd been hitting the candy canes pretty hard."

Holding tight to the gifts, Mickey took a deep breath and

climbed down into the sooty darkness. He tried humming a Christmas carol to keep up his spirits. About halfway down he paused to catch his breath. If he looked straight up he could see a beautiful big star. In the gloom, he checked the tags on Morty and Ferdie's presents.

Suddenly he panicked. The names on the cards were smudged with soot! *Now* what was he going to do?

The reindeer—they would know. Mickey started to climb back up the chimney, but he couldn't seem to move. He tried to continue going down. No luck. He was wedged, tight as could be, in the middle of the chimney. He was stuck!

"Hey up there!" he cried. "Help me! I'm stuck!"

"You can't be stuck," a reindeer answered. "Santa never gets stuck."

A pale streak of light touched the sky. All over the world, children would be waking their parents and rushing downstairs to check under the tree for their presents. And their tears of disappointment would be all Mickey's fault.

"Help me!" Mickey cried. "I'm ruining Christmas!"

Several reindeer peered into the chimney top. "Wow," one said. "He really *is* stuck."

"You shouldn't have eaten all those sugar cookies," another scolded.

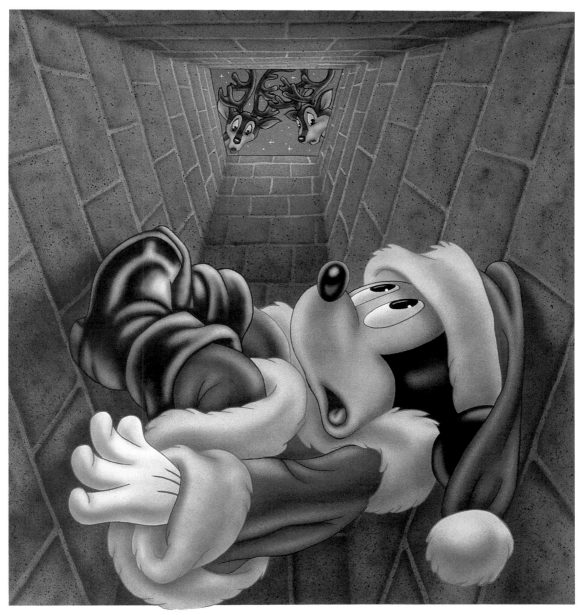

"Think about all those kids you're letting down!" a third reindeer said. "You'd better hurry, Mickey, hurry!"

"I'm coming," Mickey called. "I'm hurrying!" He struggled and squirmed, but something was pinning him in place.

"Hurry, Uncle Mickey, hurry!"

Mickey's eyes flew open. "Get me out of the chimney!" he cried.

Morty laughed. "Sure thing, Uncle Mickey," he said, nudging Ferdie. "Whatever you say."

"But—" Mickey tried to move. He looked down at his feet and saw that Pluto and Noel were lying on top of him, snoring away. "But I was filling in for Santa," he protested. "And everything was going wrong! A goat ate my map, and I got stuck in our chimney—"

Ferdie pulled on Mickey's arm. "You just had a bad dream, Uncle Mickey."

Mickey sat up. The morning sun was streaming through the curtains. The snow had finally stopped. He was home. He hadn't disappointed anyone. Christmas was safe!

With Pluto and Noel in the lead, Mickey headed downstairs. Goofy and Donald were in the living room, fast asleep on either end of the couch.

Mickey went over to the mantel. Santa's cookies were gone and the milk glass empty. A note was next to it. "Thanks for everything, Mickey," it read. "Santa. P.S.—Your present's outside."

Donald opened his eyes. "I hope you slept better than I did," he grumbled. "Goofy snored all night!"

Mickey stared at the note with a wondering smile. "Actually," he said, "I had a great night's sleep."

Morty and Ferdie's Magic Snowflake Gift Wrap

BEFORE THEY BEGIN, MORTY AND FERDIE NEED THE FOLLOWING ITEMS:

- Paper doilies (a variety of sizes is ideal)
- Large sheets of paper (newsprint, shelf paper, or brown wrapping paper all work—the thinner, the better)
- Nontoxic crayons
- Tape

HOW MORTY AND FERDIE MAKE THEIR GIFT WRAP:

1. Morty picks his favorite crayon colors and unwraps the paper covering on the crayons.

2. While Morty is busy with the crayons, Ferdie arranges several doilies in a pretty design.

3. Next, Ferdie covers the doilies with a sheet of paper. He tapes the edges of the paper down to help keep it in place.

4. Using the side of a crayon, Morty rubs gently on the paper. As he does, the outlines of the doilies magically appear like delicate snowflakes. When Morty has finished with the rubbings, Ferdie carefully removes the taped edges of the paper.

5. Together the boys wrap their presents, making sure that Donald doesn't peek!

Huey, Dewey, and Louie's Reusable Sponge-Print Gift Bags

BEFORE THEY START, HUEY, DEWEY, AND LOUIE NEED THE FOLLOWING ITEMS:

Newspaper
Plain paper grocery bags
Nontoxic water-based paint
Small containers for the paint
(margarine tubs work nicely)
Thin sponges
1 felt-tip pen
Scissors

HOW THEY MAKE THE GIFT BAGS:

1. While Huey places a thick layer of newspaper on the table, Donald pours paint into the containers and reminds the boys not to make a mess.

2. Dewey draws simple designs on sponges with a felt-tip pen. (He likes stars and Christmas trees the best.)

3. Louie (with Donald's help) cuts out the designs with a pair of scissors.

4. Each boy places a paper bag on the table and lays it flat, then carefully dips one of the sponges into the paint.

5. The boys press the sponges down on the bags gently but firmly, then carefully lift them to reveal a pretty design.

6. The boys cover their bags with sponge prints, using many different shapes and colors.   When one side is completely dry, they print the other side.

7. The top of the bag can be fringed with scissors, tied with a ribbon, or taped shut to make a wonderful, reusable sack.

$\mathcal{M}$ickey gazed contentedly at the piles of wrapping paper and mounds of ribbon scattered under his beautiful tree. Laughter filled the room like warm sunshine. All his friends who lived nearby—Daisy Duck, Clarabelle Cow, Grandma Duck, and Horace Horsecollar—had managed to make it to his house for Christmas Day by using snowshoes.

Just about the only one missing was his most special friend of all—Minnie. Under the tree sat his gift to her, a reminder that she was far away across the lake. The road to Aunt Minerva's was still deep in snow. Even with snowshoes, it was much too far for Minnie and Aunt Minerva to walk.

"Don't worry, Mickey," said Daisy. "I'm sure they'll plow the road to Aunt Minerva's soon. Minnie will be here before you know it."

Mickey smiled. "You're right, Daisy. I just hate to have her miss all this fun."

Morty, Ferdie, Huey, Dewey, and Louie came trudging in the front door from their snowball fight, bringing a blast of fresh cold air with them.

"Hey," said Morty as he brushed snow off his coat, "there are still some presents left under the tree."

"Those are Minnie's," Mickey explained with a wistful smile.

Morty knelt down to check the tags. "Nope," he said, shaking his head. "One of these says 'To Mickey, from Goofy and Donald.'"

"He was saving the best for last," said Donald, nudging Goofy.

Goofy grinned. "You'll never guess what we got you, Mickey. They're—"

Donald clamped his hand over Goofy's mouth. "Don't *tell* him! You'll ruin the surprise!"

Huey handed Mickey a red box tied with a bright silver ribbon. Mickey tore at the ribbon and paper, then lifted the top off the box. Inside were two brand-new, shiny, beautiful ice skates!

"Skates!" Mickey cried. "I always wanted my very own pair of skates!"

"It was my idea," said Goofy.

"It was *my* idea," said Donald.

"Well, thank you both," said Mickey. "It's the best Christmas present I've ever had."

He thought of his gift to Minnie—a pair of skates just like these—and sighed. "If only Minnie were here," he whispered.

"If only the lake were frozen," Clarabelle added. "Then you could try out those skates."

Ferdie and Morty exchanged grins. "Uncle Mickey?" said Ferdie, tugging on Mickey's sleeve. "We have one more present for you."

"One more?" Mickey asked in surprise. "But you already got me that great pair of earmuffs!"

"This present's even better," said Huey mischievously.

"And bigger," Dewey added.

"Much, much bigger," Louie said.

"Everybody put on your coats!" Ferdie cried.

"But why?" asked Grandma Duck. "Can't Mickey open his present in here?"

"Nope," said Morty. "We can only give it to him outside."

Mickey shrugged. "Whatever you say, boys," he said with a laugh. "Outside it is."

When everyone was bundled up in scarves and mittens and jackets and boots, the boys paused at the door. "Blindfold time," Morty announced. He tied a bright red scarf around Mickey's eyes. Then the boys led the way out the kitchen door. Morty and Ferdie held Mickey's hands. They passed Pluto's tree, which was covered with happy, well-fed birds and squirrels, and headed across the backyard, making a path in the deep snow.

When they reached the edge of the lake, Ferdie removed Mickey's blindfold. "Merry Christmas, Mickey!" the boys cried.

Mickey blinked. He didn't see a present, but he didn't want to hurt the boys' feelings. After all, they seemed so excited. Maybe this was a *pretend* present. Well, the least he could do was *pretend* to be surprised.

"Why, thank you, boys!" he said politely. "It's just what I always wanted."

Then his eyes fell on the most beautiful sight he had ever *not* seen.

Mickey gasped. The lake was gone! In its place was a smooth expanse of solid ice.

"The lake's frozen!" Mickey cried.

"Frozen?" Donald repeated. "That's impossible. It couldn't freeze overnight."

"In Junior Woodchucks, we learned it takes a long time for a lake this big to freeze," Huey said. "But I guess this lake didn't know that."

"I wonder if it's safe to cross," Mickey said.

"That's another thing we learned in Junior Woodchucks," Dewey said. "To call the police and make sure—"

"So we did," Louie interrupted excitedly, "while everyone was busy opening gifts. They said they couldn't explain it, but somehow the lake really did freeze overnight."

Mickey turned to Morty and Ferdie. "Would you boys go get my

new skates? And—oh!—my present for Minnie, too?"

Across the lake, in front of Aunt Minerva's cottage, Mickey could just make out a tiny figure waving.

"Minnie!" he cried, waving back as hard as he could. "Look, everyone! It's Minnie!"

Morty and Ferdie returned with Mickey's skates. He laced them on, grabbed Minnie's gift, and stood up hesitantly. His ankles wobbled. His blades slithered. But he was standing.

He took a tentative step onto the ice. One, two, three steps and down he went. Everyone laughed.

"Oh well," Mickey said, climbing to his feet. "If at first you don't succeed—"

"Fall, fall again," Donald finished, as Mickey plopped down.

After a few more tries, Mickey was gliding gracefully across the

ice like a pro. He turned and waved. "Thank you, boys!" he called, and then he took off across the lake.

The sun glittered on the ice. The lake shone like a huge mirror. Mickey clutched Minnie's gift. With each gliding step, she grew bigger. Soon he could make out her smiling face. With two final strokes, he skated straight into Minnie's arms.

"Mickey!" she cried, giving him a tight hug.

"Merry Christmas, Minnie!"

"I was afraid I'd miss Christmas with you," Minnie said. She stared at the lake in disbelief. "How is it possible that the lake froze overnight?"

Suddenly Mickey remembered the note from Santa on the mantel. *P.S.*, it had said. *Your present's outside.*

Could it be that Santa—? But no. That wasn't possible . . . was it?

Mickey handed Minnie her present and watched while she opened it eagerly.

"Skates!" she cried. "They're perfect!" She started to put them on, but suddenly her face fell. "But I can't leave Aunt Minerva here all alone," she said. "And there's no way she can cross the lake—not with her rheumatism."

"Wait a minute," said Mickey. "I have an idea."

Mickey took off his skates and ran to the house. While Aunt Minerva bundled up, he tied a rope to the lid of a garbage can.

He helped Aunt Minerva to the edge of the lake. "Climb on," he said. "It's a sled!"

"At my age?" said Aunt Minerva. "I couldn't possibly."

"It's Christmas," Mickey said. "Anything's possible!"

With a nervous smile, Aunt Minerva climbed onto the garbage can lid. Together, hand in hand, Mickey and Minnie skated back across the shimmering ice with the makeshift sled in tow.

"This is the only way to travel!" cried Aunt Minerva happily.

All the way across, Mickey held on tightly to Minnie's hand and didn't let go. Despite the chill in the air, he felt warm and toasty inside.

"Look at all the icicles," Minnie whispered. She pointed to the pine trees lining the lake. Long, shimmering icicles hung from their branches like frozen ornaments. "They're so beautiful. I wish we could take them inside and keep them forever!"

At last they reached the edge of the lake, where everyone was waiting. Minnie rushed to hug all her friends. The boys cheered. Pluto and Noel licked Minnie's hands.

"Who's this?" Minnie asked, laughing at the little puppy.

"That's Noel," Goofy explained. "Pluto found her."

Suddenly Pluto's ears went on alert. Noel sniffed the air nervously.

"Pluto, what's wrong?" Mickey asked.

"He probably smells food, knowing him," Donald teased.

"Uh-oh—I know what he smells, and it's not food!" Goofy said, pointing.

Everyone turned to look. Lumbering toward them across the yard were the three bears from the forest.

"Run for your lives!" Donald screeched.

"They don't *look* dangerous," Minnie whispered calmly. "In fact, they look kind of friendly."

"Those are not friendly bears," Donald told Minnie. "Trust me—we've already been introduced."

"There's something in the baby bear's mouth," Goofy said. "Something red."

Mickey's eyes widened. He had a feeling he knew what it was. He left his friends and walked slowly across the snow toward the bears. "Mickey!" Aunt Minerva called. "You be careful, young man!"

"He's the bravest fool I've ever known," Donald said, shaking his head. "Risking his life to save his friends!"

Mickey stopped. The bears came closer. Their mouths were open, and he could see their large, shiny teeth. He hoped that meant the bears were smiling at him.

For a moment the bears hesitated. The father bear sniffed the air. Mickey swallowed past a lump in his throat. He reached out his arms. "Merry Christmas, bear family!" he said in a trembling voice.

Suddenly the little cub rushed across the snow and bounded into Mickey's arms. In his mouth was Mickey's very favorite bright red hat.

"My hat!" Mickey exclaimed with relief. His hunch had been correct. "They came all this way just to bring me my hat!"

"They must have found it in the woods when it blew off," Goofy said.

Mickey stroked the little cub gently. "What a wonderful Christmas present," he said. "I wish there were some way I could say thank you."

Pluto and Noel crept over cautiously. Pluto stuck out his nose and sniffed. The bear cub sniffed back. Their noses touched.

Pluto began to wag his tail. He ran a few feet, then stopped, barking loudly. He dashed to Noel's cookie tree with Noel close behind him.

The cub climbed out of Mickey's arms and followed Pluto and Noel. He looked back at his parents questioningly. They seemed to understand. All three bears lumbered over to the tree and began to munch happily on what was left of the cookies.

Mickey put on his hat and gazed at all his friends, warmed by their smiling faces and loving hearts. "This," he said, "is the best Christmas present I could have asked for—having all of us here, all together!"

The little cub ate the last of the cookies and sighed contentedly.

"There's only one thing we have to change next Christmas," Mickey added. He smiled at Goofy and Donald. "Next year, we should bake more cookies!"

Minnie's Foil Icicle Twirls

BEFORE SHE BEGINS, MINNIE NEEDS THE FOLLOWING ITEMS:

Aluminum foil

A pencil

Ornament hangers or string

HOW MINNIE MAKES AN ICICLE:

1. Minnie rolls up a piece of aluminum foil loosely in the shape of a long tube. Then she crumples it a little with her hands.

2. Now Minnie takes her tube of foil in one hand and a pencil in her other hand. Holding the foil next to the pencil, she carefully wraps the foil around, like a snake twirling around a tree branch. (This is her favorite part.)

3. Minnie slides the pencil out. Now she makes one end of her twirly icicle pointed by pinching the end with her fingers.

4. At the top, she pokes a small hole with her pencil. Then she attaches a string or an ornament hook in the hole.

5. Minnie puts the icicle on her tree or in her window. She loves to watch it spin and sparkle as it catches the breeze.

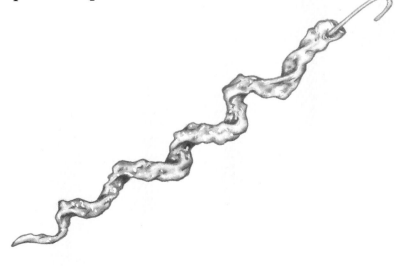